Emily ♡: Coach Katrina

One of the **HappyFeet** Kids

ISBN 13: 978-0-9992492-0-8 (Paperback)
ISBN 13: 978-0-9992492-2-2 (Hardcover)
ISBN 13: 978-0-9992492-1-5 (eBook)

Library of Congress Control Number: 2017950814

Editing by Donna Dione

Printed and bound in the United States of America.

First Printing 2017

Published by HappyFeet Books
146 Essex Street
Deep River, CT 06417

www.HappyFeetBooks.com

About HappyFeet Programs and Books

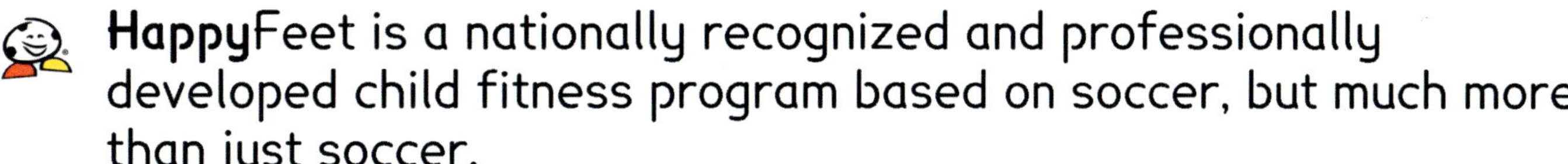

- **Happy**Feet is a nationally recognized and professionally developed child fitness program based on soccer, but much more than just soccer.

- **Happy**Feet's creative and innovative "**STORY TIME WITH A SOCCER BALL**" methodology enables children to enhance their cognitive growth, improve their balance and coordination, develop their self-confidence, and have a **BLAST** doing it!!!

- **Happy**Feet introduces children to the wonderful world of soccer, through the use of exciting, imaginary adventures with the **Happy**Feet soccer ball - **Bob the Bobcat**.

- **Happy**Feet books bring these adventures home. When parents read The **Happy**Feet Kids books to their children, the educational benefits of **Happy**Feet programming grows exponentially as fitness is combined with literacy!

- **Happy**Feet programs and **Happy**Feet books help children develop core academic skills and physical fitness in a proven, age-appropriate, and fun manner.

- Visit www.HappyFeetBooks.com to learn more.

- Visit www.HappyFeetBooks.com/locations to learn about **Happy**Feet programs near you.

THE HAPPYFEET KIDS

CREATING BRAVE, CREATIVE LEADERS, ONE STORY AT A TIME!!

*The **HappyFeet** Kids* books are based on proven **HappyFeet** class adventures, so we know kids will love them. We believe they also give parents a deeper understanding of **HappyFeet** programming. The mission of **HappyFeet** is to help children grow into brave, creative leaders for life. Our books and classes enable children to expand their imaginations and grow their motor skills in a supportive environment. The lessons learned from **HappyFeet** are retained for the rest of their lives.

On the last page of every book, you will find **HappyFeet** Soccer moves for beginner, intermediate, and advanced children. Please give them a try, and you will be combining literacy and fitness in the true **HappyFeet** spirit and developing the next brave, creative leader as a **HappyFeet** Kid!

Thank you for allowing us to help your child on this journey!!!

THE HAPPYFEET KIDS
LOAD THE TRAIN

Meet the HAPPYFEET KiDS

This is Bob the Bobcat.
He is a baby bobcat that
swallowed a magic soccer ball.
He helps the kids on their
adventures, and the kids use
their soccer skills to help Bob.

Hi, I'm Ricky. I think trains are cool and have big engines.
Hi, my name is Holly, and I like that trains have lots of cars.
Hello, my name is Sara. I like that trains have many colors.
Hello, my name is Zara, and I like that trains are strong.
Hi, I'm José, and I like that trains go fast.
HappyFeet soccer
HappyFeet soccer
HappyFeet soccer
HappyFeet soccer

Holly asked, "Coach Jan, where are we going today?"

Coach Jan explained, "The Socceropolis trains need our help."

"How can we help the trains?" José asked.

Coach Jan said, "They deliver goods from Socceropolis to places all over the world. But today the train cars are sad, because they have nothing to deliver."

Does anyone want to help me load the trains?"

The kids shouted, "I do! I do!"

Coach Jan pulled out her **Magic Stamp**. "Does anyone know what this is?"

"I do! I do!" yelled the kids.

"Anyone who is a good listener and helps me load the trains will get a **Magic Stamp**, making them strong and fast!!"

On the count of three, all the kids turned on their ears.

Suddenly, they could hear train whistles in the distance.

Coach Jan asked, “What do train engineers wear?”

Ricky said, “Boots.”

Sara said, “Overalls.”

Zara said, “Gloves.”

And Chen said, “A train hat.”

Everyone dressed in boots, overalls, gloves and a train hat.

Coach Jan asked, "How do trains move?"

Ricky answered, "On train tracks."

She had all the kids line up behind her as a train track appeared.

Coach Jan yelled, "**ALL ABOARD!**"

The group left on the tracks like a train.

Chug-a-lug! Chug-a-lug!! Choo-choo!!!

"Look, Bob the Bobcats are here. Do you think they want to help us load the trains today?" Coach Jan asked.

"**YES!**" yelled the HappyFeet Kids running to Bobs' sleeping bag.

When Coach Jan opened the bag, everyone heard the familiar sound of Bob snoring. She handed each kid a Bob. They made sure to squeeze him tight.

"Wake up Bob! We need to help the trains today!" they pleaded as they shook him. When the snoring stopped, everyone put Bob on the ground.

To see if he was really awake, each kid touched Bob with their fingers. They yelped when Bob the Bobcat took a little nibble. They stepped on Bob and said, "**Stop Bob!**" He did not bite.

Coach Jan confessed, "I forgot to clean the train boots. They must be really stinky - pee-yew. He won't bite our feet today."

The HappyFeet Kids dribbled Bob to the train station, where they saw the Blue Car, the Yellow Car, and the Red Car lined up on the train track.

The train cars said, “We are all sad because we have no goods to deliver from Socceropolis today. Can you help us please?”

Holly asked, “How can we help you?”

The **Blue Car** said, "I need to be loaded with milk."

Coach Jan asked the kids, "Who gives us milk?"

"**COWS**!!!" they shouted.

Off to the farm they went, dribbling their Bobs and chanting, "Come with me Bob!"

At the farm, Sara asked, “What should we collect the milk in?”

Chen answered, “A milk bucket.”

Everyone grabbed a bucket.

SQUIRT, **SQUIRT**, **SQUIRT** the milk! By doing tippy-toes on their Bobs, the HappyFeet Kids filled the buckets with milk.

Picking up their buckets, they said, "Back to the train, Bob."

At the station, they lined up the buckets on the **Blue Car**. "I have **MILK!** I have **MILK!**" laughed the **Blue Car**.

The HappyFeet Kids were glad they had helped, and they left the **Blue Car** with a big smile on her face.

The Yellow Car said, “I need to be loaded with wood.”

“Where do we get wood from?” asked Coach Jan.

“**TREES!**” answered the kids.

“Come on Bob!” they said, dribbling him to the forest.

The kids helped Bob saw into the trees by doing tick-tocks.

Soon, **CREEEEK, CREEEEK, CREEEEK,**
could be heard coming from the trees.

Then the kids kicked Bob
into the trees.

"**TIMBER!**"
they yelled
as the trees fell.

The kids picked up the wood and took it back to the **Yellow Car**, where they lined it up on the car, just like the milk.

The **Yellow Car** was so happy that she cried, “Thank you.”

The kids were happy too. It was fun to help the trains.

Then the Red Car said, "I need to be loaded with mail."

Coach Jan did not know how to help the Red Car, so she asked, "Where can we get mail?"

Ricky said, "I don't know."

Sara asked, "From the post office?"

But the post office was closed. It was starting to look like the kids were not going to be able to help the Red Car.

Suddenly, Zara exclaimed, "I have an idea!!! Let's wrap some toys as presents and have the Red Car mail them!"

The HappyFeet Kids dribbled to the toy store saying, "Come with me Bob."

They asked the toy maker if he had any toys they could wrap for the **Red Car** to mail. The toy maker handed each kid a toy. Coach Jan gave them a sheet of wrapping paper. The kids put the toy in Bob's mouth and the paper on their feet.

Then the kids used one of their favorite soccer skills, **the step-over**, to wrap the toy. "Stand next to Bob - tap your foot far from Bob - that foot goes in front (Whoosh) - the other foot goes behind (Whoop)," called Coach Jan.

"One, two, three, Boing!" the kids yelled as they jumped over Bob to tie the ribbon around the box.

They dribbled their Bob, who was still holding the wrapped toy in his mouth, back to the Red Car.

They piled all the wrapped toys on the Red Car. "You are so helpful," beamed the Red Car.

The HappyFeet Kids knew they had done their best to be helpful all day. They all cheered as the train chugged down the tracks to the rest of the world, loaded with milk buckets, wood, and wrapped toys for mail.

The Bobs were tired after helping the train cars all day. The HappyFeet Kids sang *Rock-a-bye-Bobcat* as they rocked them to sleep.

Once they heard snoring, they knew it was safe to pick up their Bob and put him back in his sleeping bag.

The HappyFeet Kids then followed Coach Jan back to their secret hideout, where she pulled out her **Magic Stamp** and said, "I'm so proud of you for being such good listeners."

After each kid received their stamp, they showed her their strong muscles and their fast feet.

Each kid gave Coach Jan a **BIG, STRONG HIGH FIVE!!!**

"How did you get so strong?" she asked.

The kids all laughed, because they knew it was the magic making them strong – good listening strong.

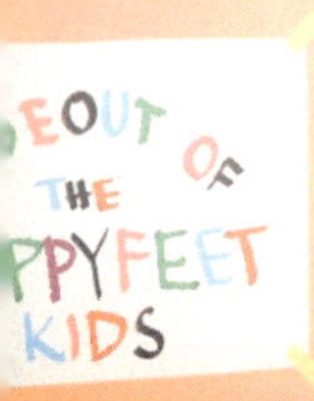

Before going home, the HappyFeet Kids and Coach Jan all put their hands in the middle. Coach Jan asked, "Was it fun to help the trains today?"

"**YES!**" yelled the kids.

She asked, "Would it be fun to help someone else today?"

"**YES!**" cheered the kids.

"Fantastic! Leaders always have fun helping others," exclaimed Coach Jan.

Coach Jan counted, "one, **two,** **three!**"

"WE LOVE HAPPYFEET!!!"

HAPPYFEET SOCCER SKILLS

Beginner Tippy Toes

Left foot on Bob | Right foot on Bob | Left foot on Bob

Intermediate Moving Tick-Tocks

Walk and move Bob back and forth with inside of feet

Advanced Step-Over

Tap right foot-right foot in front of Bob, right foot on ground (legs crossed)-left foot behind Bob-left foot on ground-push Bob away with outside of right foot

Made in the USA
San Bernardino, CA
19 October 2018